Mona Khademi, in conjunction with her professional work, has written and presented research papers at international conferences and has published some of them in books, academic journals, and magazines in Persian and English.

Ms. Khademi has a bachelor's degree in psychology from Pahlavi (currently Shiraz) University, Iran, and a master's degree from American University in Washington, D.C. She has worked towards a PhD at Imperial College of London.

Contents

Foreword

This small but rich compilation includes reminiscences of four inflamed lovers of 'Abdu'l-Bahá who spent a period of their lives in the presence of their Beloved and then beautified the pages of history with their memories. While it was easy to feel enamored with these sweet stories and anecdotes, it was a painstaking task to choose selections from hundreds of fascinating stories to include in this collection. In these pages, the Master's distinguished moral qualities and the characteristics of His everyday life are vividly captured, which is naturally of much greater value than just stating that He had specific qualities.

I had the privilege of presenting portions of this research paper at a Bahá'í conference on 'Abdu'l-Bahá, and later I shared some of the sweet reminiscences in Persian and English at several Bahá'í schools, conferences, and other gatherings. In response to requests and the encouragement of many friends present at these events, I prepared and edited the

Persian version as a compilation, which was published in early 2012. The English one now follows with some additional material added, which I humbly offer to the faithful followers of 'Abdu'l-Bahá and those who are exploring His life and deeds.

I would like to take this opportunity to thank those individuals who assisted me. First and foremost, they include my dear grandfather, Dr. Habib Moayyad, who taught me to love and respect 'Abdu'l-Bahá. I will always be indebted to my beloved mother, Ms. Bahieh Moayyad-Khademi, who was a source of encouragement and support several years ago when I first started working on this paper. Also, I am grateful to my father, Ali Mohammad Khademi, who set the example of faith, dedication, and service when I had him in my life.

Dr. Shapour Rassekh, who did not withhold from lending any assistance or guidance, has my deep gratitude, as does Shabnam Moinipour, who helped in translating Badi Bushrui's accounts and other parts of this compilation. My gratitude goes to Dr. Khazeh Fananapazir for translation of an account and reviewing the manuscript as well as to Dr. Moojan Momen and Sheila Wolcott-Banani for their assistance in reviewing the book. I am also deeply indebted to the invaluable assistance of Eileen Maddocks in editing my manuscript and improving the final version.

All those individuals who made their valuable memoirs available to the Bahá'í world have our profound appreciation.

I am immensely delighted that this collection is being

published during the centenary celebrations of 'Abdu'l-Bahá's journeys to the West. It is hoped that the reader will gain a deeper understanding of the teachings of the Bahá'í Faith through the example of 'Abdu'l-Bahá and that this compilation will become a bridge for greater appreciation of His station.

Mona Khademi
Washington, D.C.

Introduction

There are many ways of looking at the life, station, and legacy of 'Abdu'l-Bahá, son of Bahá'u'lláh, the Prophet-Founder of the Bahá'í Faith, and numerous books and articles illustrate them.[1] One way to learn about the life of 'Abdu'l-Bahá, who was designated by Bahá'u'lláh as the Center of His Covenant, is by reading the records of His addresses and utterances, and another is by reading the biographies of Him. Still another manner of celebrating His legacy is by the frequent retelling of stories about His encounters with a diverse array of people. Such accounts have significance as inspirational literature because they tell us what his words and actions meant to those who experienced them. These anecdotal stories provide an illuminating context for the study of 'Abdu'l-Bahá's personality and character.

Scores of Bahá'ís from the East and the West attained the presence of 'Abdu'l-Bahá. Eastern Bahá'ís had various opportunities to go on pilgrimage to the prison city of 'Akká, Palestine, to meet with Bahá'u'lláh and 'Abdu'l-Bahá from the early years of their imprisonment.[2] Western Bahá'ís started making pilgrimages to see the Master in 'Akká in 1898, and the numbers increased after He moved to Haifa, Palestine, soon after. However, most of His western followers did not meet the Master until He traveled to the West, and some of the westerners only became followers after meeting Him and thereafter wrote their accounts. Several of these devoted believers recorded their memories of those visits, and each of these unique memoirs will be valuable for eternity.

Some of the individuals who met 'Abdu'l-Bahá wrote of everyday events that occurred when in His presence, while others recorded His talks, remarks, and addresses. Others recounted the manner and personality of that exceptional being. Some of these memories were recorded daily in diaries while others beautified the pages of memoirs after a lapse of time.

Examples of these priceless memoirs of people from the East and the West include: *Memories of Nine Years in 'Akká* by Dr. Youness Afroukhteh; *Mahmúd's Diary*, two volumes by Mírzá Mahmúd-i-Zarqání; *Khátirát-i Habíb* (The Diary of Habib) by Dr. Habib Moayyad; the unpublished memoirs of Mirza Badi Bushrui; *'Abdu'l-Bahá in America: Agnes Parsons' Diary* by Agnes Parsons; *The Diary of Juliet Thompson* by Juliet Thompson; *The Chosen Highway* by Lady Blomfield; *Portals to Freedom* by Howard Colby Ives;

An Early Pilgrimage by May Maxwell; and *Memories of 'Abdu'l-Bahá: Recollections of the Early Days of the Bahá'í Faith in California* by Ramona Allen Brown.[3]

As to the importance of the memoirs of those who were privileged to meet the head of the Faith, they are more likely to be close to their original form than the ones that were only preserved verbally.[4] Written memoirs "tell us what his words and actions meant to those who witnessed them. Although such accounts may well contain historical inaccuracies, they form an intriguing body of sacred stories, vignettes in which those who had the privilege of coming into the Master's presence render their experiences."[5]

These memoirs are not to be considered as authoritative sources and should not be used to support definitive answers to theological and religious subjects. They were written from personal memories in accordance with various levels of interpretive ability of their authors. But they all contain spiritual and moral lessons that are inspiring and extend the sweet savors of 'Abdu'l-Bahá's lofty words and deeds for His followers. These memoirs should be seen as an important source that must be supplemented by other accounts of the Master's words, character, and life if a complete and accurate portrayal of the Master is to be depicted. There are numerous books that portray at length 'Abdu'l-Bahá's life and ministry, his spiritual qualities and characteristics.

Attributes of the Master have been summarized by a Bahá'í scholar as follows:

Universal affection and mercy, attention and paternal care of the needy, awareness and wide - ranging knowledge of history, amazing vision of the future, infinite spirituality and reliance on God, absolute love and pure servitude towards the Blessed Beauty [Bahá'u'lláh], humility and selflessness, extraordinary forbearance in the face of calamities and hardships, service to the Divine Threshold [Bahá'u'lláh] and to humanity, exceptional power of speech and delivery, sense of humour, pleasant character and good temper, immense affection towards children, and last but not least, enormous intellectual capacity and tireless power.[6]

How did the Master demonstrate the principles He was teaching in His daily life? In this compilation, anecdotes are selected from four memoirs recounting the attributes and qualities of 'Abdu'l-Bahá through His deeds. It is perhaps more important to show how these traits were manifested from His blessed soul rather than just mentioning them.

The four dedicated souls whose memoirs are chosen for this compilation, in the order that their stories are presented, are: Mirza Badi Bushrui, an Arab of Iranian descent; Dr. Habib Moayyad, an Iranian; Lady Sara Louisa Blomfield, an Irish woman living in England; and Howard Colby Ives, an American. They were in the presence of 'Abdu'l-Bahá at different stages of their lives. Mirza Badi Bushrui met

'Abdu'l-Bahá during childhood, Dr. Habib Moayyad during his youth, Lady Blomfield and Howard Colby Ives at more mature age. Each of the four devotees' memoirs is presented according to when the person first met 'Abdu'l-Bahá. However, the anecdotes selected in each section are told in no particular order, although the selections are presented as quotes and as they appear in the respective memoirs, with no changes. The narratives recounted by these two Easterners and two Westerners—three men and one woman—illustrate many of the exceptional traits and attributes of the Master.

It is noteworthy that each anecdote has its own unique style and angle of perspective, which give this volume an appealing diversity as it presents firsthand stories of attaining the presence of 'Abdu'l-Bahá. Each individual recorded memories of Him with his own spiritual and physical eyes, preserving what he felt was important. It becomes apparent that each writer found in 'Abdu'l-Bahá what he most longed for, as each narrative reveals the sensibilities of its author. However, the reader must be reminded that all of these portrayals are taken out of the contexts of the books in which they were published. In addition, these accounts are all from the last twenty years of 'Abdu'l-Bahá's life.

After a short introduction of 'Abdu'l-Bahá, each of the four authors is introduced, and each introduction is then followed by stories selected from memoirs that clearly reflect attributes manifested by 'Abdu'l-Bahá.[7]

'Abdu'l-Bahá

'Abdu'l-Bahá was born on May 23, 1844, in Tehran, Iran, and was given the name 'Abbas after his grandfather. He later adopted the title of 'Abdu'l-Bahá (Servant of the Glory of God) and was commonly referred to as "the Master" by His followers. From childhood, 'Abdu'l-Bahá shared his Father's sufferings and accompanied Him in numerous banishments. He was eight years old when His Father Bahá'u'lláh was imprisoned for His religious views and the family's possessions were looted, leaving the family in virtual poverty.

In 1853, Bahá'u'lláh and His family were first exiled by the decree of the Shah of Iran to Baghdad, Iraq, where the family lived for nine years. Then by the decree of the Ottoman Empire, they were exiled to Constantinople, Turkey, then to Adrianople, Turkey, and finally to 'Akká, Palestine, when 'Abdu'l-Bahá was 24. After Bahá'u'lláh's passing in

1892 and according to His will, 'Abdu'l-Bahá was appointed as His successor, the head of the Bahá'í Faith, and the authorized interpreter of His Father's Writings. In addition, Bahá'ís regard him as the Perfect Exemplar of a Bahá'í life.

'Abdu'l-Bahá's imprisonment in Palestine lasted until 1908, when He was freed at age 64 by the Young Turks

Revolution. Only then could He and His family begin to live in relative safety.

'Abdu'l-Bahá was called the "prophet of peace," a man who "walked the mystical path with practical feet."[8] Edward G. Browne, the renowned Orientalist, wrote the following after meeting 'Abdu'l-Bahá:

> Subsequent conversation with him served only to heighten the respect with which his appearance had from the first inspired me. One more eloquent of speech, more ready of argument, more apt of illustration, more intimately acquainted with the sacred books of the Jews, the Christians, and the Muhammadans, could, I should think, scarcely be found even amongst the eloquent, ready, and subtle race to which he belongs. These qualities, combined with a bearing at once majestic and genial, made me cease to wonder at the influence and esteem which he enjoyed even beyond the circle of his father's followers. About the greatness of this man and his power no one who had seen him could entertain a doubt.[9]

'Abdu'l-Bahá's journeys to Egypt and the West from 1910 to 1913 helped spread the Bahá'í message beyond its middle-eastern roots. His life of service came to an end in Palestine (today's Israel) in 1921.

Mirza Badi Bushrui

The first devout follower whose memories of 'Abdu'l-Bahá are presented here is Mirza Badi Bushrui, who was given the distinctive title "Badi Effendi" by 'Abdu'l-Bahá.[10] He was the youngest of the four chosen devotees for this compilation, having been ten years old when he was showered by 'Abdu'l-Bahá's mercy and grace.[11] Mirza Badi Bushrui was born on December 15, 1892, at Bushruyih in the province of Khurásán, Iran. He entered his first school in Ishqábád and lost his father at a young age. Then circumstances "ordained that his well of filial love and devotion should flow to a new 'father'—'Abdu'l-Bahá."[12] At the age of ten, he arrived in the Holy Land and was under the special care of 'Abdu'l-Bahá. He describes his first meeting with the Master and memories of his childhood years in this way:

> As I climbed the stairs of the house of the Master and reached the Master's room, I was swooned by the life-sustaining melodies of "welcome, welcome." As my eyes beheld His

elegant countenance, I lost all consciousness .
. . 'Abdu'l-Bahá had a kind and merciful
regard for this feeble one, and the hospitality
of the Greatest Holy Leaf [Bahíyyih Khánum,
sister of 'Abdu'l-Bahá], opened the doors of
happiness and joy from every side . . . The
blessing of being a child drew the attention of
Shoghi Effendi[13] towards this insignificant
being and I was called "the little traveller."
Most of the time, be it during playtime or
visits to the Shrine of Bahá'u'lláh, I was
privileged to be in His presence. 'Abdu'l-Bahá
ordered me to write my homework in Persian
under the supervision of Mishkín-Qalam and
to learn reading in Persian and English.[14]

Badi Effendi resided in the Holy Land for three years, left
for one year, and then returned. With 'Abdu'l-Bahá's
encouragement, he pursued a university education at the
Syrian Protestant College (later named the American
University) in Beirut, Lebanon.[15] Upon his return to Haifa,
Bushrui wrote the following:

The eight-year period at the American
University in Beirut came to an end and the
star of hope and the desire to reach the
illuminating presence of Him whom God hath
willeth became permanently radiant. . . . in
short, I entered the sanctuary of the Friend
['Abdu'l-Bahá] and bowed down my head at
the threshold of the Beloved and, without any
worth or merit, and my eyes and heart were

enlightened by the matchless beauty of the
Master. The ocean of bounty and mercy was
surging. This dust was honoured and accepted
by Him to His holy threshold and was housed
and sheltered in the Pilgrim House on Mount
Carmel at the service of the foremost follower
of the Centre of the Covenant, Mirzá Haydar-
'Ali.[16]

At the beginning of World War I, 'Abdu'l-Bahá had sent the
believers who were living in Haifa to the Druze village of
Abu Sinan located east of 'Akká for their protection and
safety. Bushrui was to run a school there for the Bahá'í
children while Dr. Moayyad took charge of the dispensary.[17]
The two young men labored under the supervision of the
Greatest Holy Leaf, 'Abdu'l-Bahá's sister and faithful
companion.

Bushrui subsequently spent 30 years in Palestine in religious and governmental service until 1948, when he settled in Alexandria, Egypt, with his family, as advised by Shoghi Effendi. He continued to be a faithful servant of the Faith in Egypt until his death.

'Abdu'l-Bahá had once told Bushrui, "Badi Effendi, I need you for a great cause in the future."[18] Years later, during the period when the Cause of God was under severe hardship in Egypt, Bushrui rendered numerous services and nurtured the Bahá'ís in Egypt. Bushrui passed away from this mortal world in 1973 at the age of 81. He left his observations and conversations in a memoir titled "The Nineteen Years of Happiness in the Promised Land," which is a valuable and rich treasure.

Memories of Mirza Badi Bushrui

This section starts with an anecdote recorded early by Bushrui with regard to the difficulties and hardships endured by 'Abdu'l-Bahá during His imprisonment in 'Akká. He writes:

> Anywhere that He looked, He saw nothing but the military fortress with its thick crenulated walls armed with cannons and guards. Watchmen constantly scrutinized every entrance to and exit from the fortress. There were two parallel ditches deep dug to prevent entry. It was clear and evident that all these precautions had been taken to curtail the freedom of some of the inhabitants of this fortified city. In addition, it could be observed that 'Abdu'l-Bahá was not free to travel outside the fortress. He was even deprived of

visiting Bahá'u'lláh's resting place, His sole
consolation after Bahá'u'lláh's passing. Every
time He glanced at the place of martyrdom of
Mírzá Mihdí, the Purest Branch, which was
located steps away from the prison cell of
Bahá'u'lláh, He would be deeply moved. All
of these various sites would greatly affect
every atom in His body.[19] At any point in
time, the glimpse of such a sight of import
would engrave another picture on the pages of
His heart.[20]

The Master paid special attention to the education of
children, as is evident in this account:

> In those days, as per orders of 'Abdu'l-Bahá, a
> small school was established in a room
> adjacent to the Pilgrim House in Haifa for
> about 15 youth and children of the
> believers. . . . Usually on Fridays, the students
> of the school gathered in the House of the
> Master . . . and stood in a row, holding their
> handwritings while 'Abdu'l-Bahá looked at
> them one by one and, with absolute kindness
> and interest, encouraged them with fatherly
> affection. Besides showering His bounties and
> mercies upon the students, He would give gifts
> to some. Unfortunately, because of complaints
> of the Covenant-breakers and enemies of the
> Faith, the school was closed in 1904 by order
> of the Sultan.[21]

In addition, the Master's attention to the moral education of children was clearly witnessed. Bushrui writes this anecdote dated August 3, 1915:

> While walking, as He would look either at the sea or the mountains or the barren areas, He would shower us with His utterances. Once He stated: "How wonderful it would have been if a House of Worship and a Bahá'í school had been built on this mountain. People do not realize the magnificence of a Bahá'í school; otherwise everyone would wish the establishment of a good school with high standards of spirituality that would immensely serve the world of learning."[22]

In another story, 'Abdu'l-Bahá's awareness of future happenings is clearly noted. Bushrui writes of such an episode that occurred in Haifa dated June 4, 1916:

> One afternoon, while in a carriage riding to the top of Mt. Carmel, He admired the fine weather and pleasant view. He went to a German hotel which is situated at the foot of the Mt. Carmel. . . . There were many spruce and pine trees on the southern side of the hotel. He walked under the trees and talked about the benefits of such trees and their effect on the climate. He continued His walk on the semi-barren mountain slope until He reached a monument erected to commemorate the visit of an Emperor of Germany. He paused there

and gazed at the beautiful scenery. Then, He mentioned the development of the mountain. He said: "God willing, the Bahá'ís will develop this mountain. . . . All these lands will become the property of the Bahá'ís. This will not occur in Our lifetime but you (He pointed at us) will see it. We laid the foundations for the Shrine of the Báb and the Pilgrim House."[23]

'Abdu'l-Bahá faced many difficulties and persecutions during His lifetime. However, the outpouring of divine confirmations was continual, an example of which Bushrui recorded on July 20, 1914, as follows:

The Beloved ['Abdu'l-Bahá] went to the Shrine of the Báb and, after being seated, He talked about the construction of the Shrine of the Báb and the hardships endured by His auspicious being which caused His physical weakness and fragility.[24] One reason for this hardship was the lack of a proper path to the Shrine because of the strictness of the Russian consul, through whose land a road needed to go. After grave hardships and disappointments while endeavouring to find a solution to this problem, He went to a room by Himself, closed the door, and recited a verse of the Báb until a divine door was opened and the issue was resolved. He then said: "It is a wonder that people do not yet repent. Some have become trapped. For example, 'Abdul-

Rahmán Pasha wanted to close down the shops of the Bahá'ís and confine me. One early morning, he was ready to carry out his plans when a telegraph from Istanbul was received that stated he had been fired from his post and was replaced by someone else. Then the investigating committee came and kissed the hands of 'Abbás Effendi!"[25]

There are many accounts concerning the attention that 'Abdu'l-Bahá gave to the needy and poor. He has recorded this story of July 27, 1915:

At an event, the poor were mentioned and the fact that there is much hunger in Beirut and that some people grind bones and eat the powdered bones! He ['Abdu'l-Bahá] said: "The rich have no mercy upon the poor. They, themselves, are also vanquished. If they had mercy, both the rich and the poor could be in comfort. This kind of fellowship must be applied in such cases so that the rich and the poor console one another. There is no greater harm to the rich than having resources and wealth while the poor are needy and abased. In Isfahan, when the great famine happened and the dead were taken out of their graves and eaten and people were dying in the streets, the King of Martyrs did not let even one believer go hungry or turn to others [for food]."[26]

The kindness and generosity of 'Abdu'l-Bahá' were well known. Bushrui writes:

> On one occasion, Baghdad was mentioned and He ['Abdu'l-Bahá] stated: "In Baghdad we had only one rug, the rest of the carpets were made of straw mat. One day a firewood seller sat on the rug after long and tiresome travel and said: 'Lucky the person who sits and rests on this rug.' I told him to take this rug for himself. He was in awe and thought that I was joking. Since I insisted, he took the rug and as he was leaving, he kept looking back lest someone take the rug away from him."[27]

The Master was also noted as saying:

> Always bear in mind to help the poor and the needy. To the extent that is possible, help members of every nationality and every tribe. Do not be like those people who, after giving assistance, make the poor and the needy indebted to themselves. You have to be indebted to the poor for their acceptance of your help.[28]

Another entry in Bushrui's memoirs states:

> The poor have swarmed around Him and for the Master it is too hard to turn them away disappointed. Today, He borrowed twenty liras and was continuously giving it out to the poor.[29]

With regards to the Master's gentleness and his attachment to nature, Bushrui observed:

> In His holy home, which was 'Abdulláh Páshá's residence, . . . He looked at the delicate and colourful flowers and immensely enjoyed watching the flight of beautiful butterflies from flower to flower. He took delight in the singing of the nightingales and the sweet melodies of birds. It was observed that at the Shrine of Bahá'u'lláh, . . . 'Abdu'l-Bahá would carry water and soil on His shoulders, in uttermost humility and lowliness, to the garden adjacent to the Shrine of Bahá'u'lláh. Pilgrims and companions all took part in this pious act.[30]

Bushrui also recounts:

> He had asked for narcissus bulbs to be brought for planting in the garden of the Shrine of Bahá'u'lláh. Right after sunset, He asked the gardeners to come the next day to plant them so that they would blossom in time for the first day of Muharram.[31]

This faithful follower also has recorded the following:

> He arose and started walking in the garden and, since it had rained, the trees, flowers, and plants manifested renewed freshness and delicacy. While observing, He said: "Every page of this creation is a true book and each of these things reveals a hidden mystery of the

world of nature; it needs a seeing eye to
behold and observe."[32]

In another episode, Bushrui illustrates a clear example of
the Master's interest in reciting with His delightful voice the
lyrical poems of Bahá'u'lláh. He records:

> On the way from Haifa to 'Akká, the Master
> asked Aqá Mirzá Ahmad: "Can you chant?
> Chant one of Bahá'u'lláh's lyrical poems." In
> turn, one by one, Aqá Mirzá Ahmad, Ustád
> Muhammad 'Ali, and this servant [Badi
> Bushrui] chanted loudly and sometimes the
> Master Himself would accompany us,
> interpreting and expounding on the meaning
> of some of the poems.[33]

The next anecdote confirms the Master's humility on one
hand and on the other the divine confirmations that are
bestowed upon those individuals who teach His Cause.
Bushrui stated the following on July 13, 1915:

> On one occasion, the Master mentioned the
> Hindus and said: "They went to America and
> gave good speeches and they were skilled, too.
> Even though they knew English well, they did
> not achieve much. But We sent the mutes and
> progress was made. Before I went to Europe, I
> had not given any speeches because it is not
> customary in the East. But I found myself
> immersed in the ocean of speech. This is like
> someone who goes to war alone but receives

regiments from behind. Now each and every Bahá'í who travels in any direction will receive a multitude of confirmations. This is why Jesus told His Apostles, 'I am with you. Be confident, the Holy Spirit confirms you in time of teachings, do not think; just speak out what comes to your heart.'"[34]

'Abdu'l-Bahá always emphasized reliance upon and faith in Bahá'u'lláh and His confirmations. After His return from His journeys to West in 1912, He said:

> This travel to America caused much inconvenience; it took a few years. Every day we were on the move to a place but the divine power and confirmations were clear and evident. For example, in one place, weakness and fever was such that there was no strength to move. As soon as We went on, that health condition changed; weakness and fever went away and strength came back until We reached home. . . . I would talk for one hour, the confirmations of Bahá'u'lláh would pour forth. If it had not been for the confirmations of the Blessed Beauty [Bahá'u'lláh], I could not have borne the hardships and difficulties of this travel even for one day.[35]

At the end of this section, some short anecdotes are shared:

> The Master was not feeling well. He said: "I move even in this condition so that the

believers would see how I efface myself in Him [Bahá'u'lláh] and learn from it."[36]

In another place, he states:

He was seated in the courtyard of the house for a while and spoke of different matters; these were mainly funny stories.[37]

Here is another story dated November 21, 1915:

In the morning, He quickly came out and started walking in the garden. A telegraph was received from Simon Effendi, the head of Customs in 'Akká, who had stated that "my daughter is unwell and I want her to come to the House of the Master in Haifa for a few days in order to recover." Addressing Aqá Dádáshi, 'Abdu'l-Bahá said, "Look as to what the Bahá'ís have done to make this man have such trust to send his daughter to us, even though he is a Christian."[38]

In addition, Bushrui reminds us of 'Abdu'l-Bahá's service to the Bahá'ís by writing this short recollection:

An individual told Him ['Abdu'l-Bahá] that Háji [Muhammad] used to serve the Bahá'ís a great deal in Beirut. He ['Abdu'l-Bahá] responded: "This is his honor. It is our honor to serve the Bahá'ís."[39]

Bushrui also notes the faith 'Abdu'l-Bahá had that material needs would be met. He states:

While gazing at the Shrine of the Báb, He stated: "The Shrine of the Báb did not get finished; it needs ten to twenty thousand liras. God willing, it will happen. We have gotten it this far."[40]

The sweet and captivating stories of Bushrui are many, and choosing only a few for the purposes of this book was no easy task.

Dr. Habib Moayyad

The next devout follower whose memories are recounted here is Mirzá Habíbu'lláh [Habib] Khudábakhsh, who was given the name "Mú'ayyad" [Moayyad], meaning "confirmed," by 'Abdu'l-Bahá. He was born in 1888 in Kermanshah, Iran.[41] His father was Mirza Khudábakhsh, one of the early believers during the time of Bahá'u'lláh. Mirza Habib received his elementary education in Kermanshah and continued his education at the American School in Hamadan, Iran.[42] His father, Khudábakhsh, was an intoxicated lover of the Cause of Bahá'u'lláh. When Khudábakhsh's eldest son, Murád, was martyred, he went to the man who had put an end to his son's life and kissed his hand.[43]

At the age of 19 in October 1907, Mirza Habib went to the Holy Land, where he spent a month absorbing wisdom from 'Abdu'l-Bahá. Although he had been planning to proceed to the United Sates to further his studies, with the

approval of the Master he went to Beirut, where he started medical school at the Syrian Protestant College. The Master had told him: "Since Iran needs doctors, the most praiseworthy and preferred is that you study in the medical field." Therefore, Mirza Habib pursued the field of medicine.[44] During this period of his studies, he served various Bahá'í communities and extended hospitality to visitors and pilgrims. While studying in Beirut, his bounty was the privilege of visiting 'Abdu'l-Bahá in the Holy Land during the summers and in

catching glimpses of His infinite wisdom and knowledge. When 'Abdu'l-Bahá departed for Europe and America, Mirza Habib was the intermediary used for the dispatch of the Master's tablets and telegrams.[45] He also had the honor of rendering personal services to Mirzá Abu'l Fádl and participating in the activities of the Bahá'ís of Beirut.[46]

'Abdu'l-Bahá, in one of His Tablets referring to that period of Habib's life, wrote how his presence among the students of Beirut vivified them like the flowers and plants in a garden and that he engaged in increasing love and fellowship among them through piety and detachment. Because of his love of the Cause of God, he made the fresh and verdant flowers to seem as lush gardens.[47]

Mirza Habib graduated as a physician from the Syrian Protestant College in 1914, returned to Haifa, and at the request of the Master traveled with Azizu'lláh Bahádor throughout Germany to meet with dignitaries and the Bahá'ís the same year.[48] When World War I broke out, the Master recalled them to Haifa.

Mirza Habib operated a dispensary that was open to Bahá'ís and non-Bahá'ís alike in the Druze village of Abu Sinan, to where the Master had evacuated the Bahá'ís who had been living in 'Akká and Haifa.[49] Lua Getsinger, an early American Bahá'í, recalls assisting "a young Persian physician – who graduated from the American College in Bayreuth" by giving anesthetics for him at this dispensary.[50] Although troubles raged around the small Bahá'í community, Dr. Moayyad was often heard to say in later years that "this time spent near 'Abdu'l-Bahá and the Greatest Holy Leaf was among the sweetest, most precious and memorable segments" of his life.[51]

The Master revealed a Tablet in which He praised Dr. Moayyad for being "confirmed."[52] Referring to his years in Beirut, He also stated that with his deep and sacrificial devotion, Moayyad did everything that he could for the friends of God.[53]

After a few months stay in Haifa, Dr. Habib was instructed to proceed to Persia. Upon his departure, 'Abdu'l-Bahá addressed a Tablet to Habib's father stating, in effect, that he should thank God for such a "worthy son" and describing him as a "lamp enkindled with the love of God" and as one "engaged in the service of humanity."[54] The father would, the Master wrote, "infinitely rejoice in beholding his countenance, in inhaling the fragrances of his presence."[55]

Upon his return to Persia, Dr. Moayyad started a family and initiated his medical career serving dignitaries as well as the poor. He was later awarded the title of Rafi'ul-Mamálik (The Nobleman of the Realm) by Ahmad Shah.[56] He continued his correspondence with the Master and later with Shoghi Effendi.

Dr. Moayyad's sweet and charming memoirs, with notes of his daily observations, were published at the request of Shoghi Effendi. Dr. Moayyad writes:

> It should not elude men of insight that it was in my youth that I was granted the privilege of attaining the presence of His Holiness 'Abdu'l-Bahá. At that time, I was neither overly concerned with spiritual issues or with matters pertaining to the world hereafter. My sole desire was to behold the luminous countenance of the Master and, in a state of rapture, listen to Him speak. Hence, being unaware of their future significance, the notes I kept were very abbreviated, intended

principally to aid me to remember the events of those days and the sweetness and joy of being in His presence. With pen or pencil, I recorded the essence of whatever, I perceived to be important or beneficial in a small pocketbook that I always carried with me. Therefore the utterances of 'Abdu'l-Bahá [presented in this diary] are not His exact words but, rather, what I recalled after I had returned to the pilgrim house, when I committed them to paper, often using my own inadequate expressions.[57]

These memoirs not only have the sweet utterances of 'Abdu'l-Bahá but they also describe Dr. Moayyad's own personal feelings and expressions. They were made available in Persian in two volumes for the lovers and devotees of 'Abdu'l-Bahá. Dr. Moayyad left this mortal world in Tehran in 1971.[58]

Memories of Dr. Habib Moayyad

Moayyad's memoirs open with an overview of his notes concerning the vision, attitudes, and personal characteristics of 'Abdu'l-Bahá, especially in His relationships with those who sought his counsel. After discussing the diversity of the people—their various races, religions, and strata of life, Easterners and Westerners, Arabs and Jews, Bahá'ís and non-Bahá'ís—who visited Him and asked His counsel, Habib Moayyad writes:

> In short, hundreds of people attained His sacred presence, and each had his own questions and inquired about matters that interested him, whether in the field of religion, science, or spirituality. In every instance, they would depart from 'Abdu'l-Bahá's presence with the utmost joy and tranquility, praising

and glorifying Him. They were all captivated by His charm and personality and considered Him an utmost expert and authority in their field of interest.

In addition to such inquirers, there were many with material needs and difficulties [who] approached 'Abdu'l-Bahá with hope of a solution. Whatever their troubles or material worries, or problems with adversaries in the governmental agencies or the military establishment, they considered the Master to be their sole support and confidant.

In turn, with utmost compassion, He would listen to their problems, heed their requests, solve their difficulties, and, with words of encouragement and comfort, send them away happy and hopeful. When poets, scholars, scientists, and men of letters attained 'Abdu'l-Bahá's presence, they would instinctively begin to extol and exalt the Center of the Covenant. In particular, Arab poets-whether Muslim, Druze, or Christian-would spontaneously compose elegant verses extolling the Master.[59] At times, their poems exhibited the highest degree of eloquence and beauty, and were read by them in the presence of 'Abdu'l-Bahá and then decorated and given to Him with great respect. He always graciously received such papers and when they [the visitors] had left, [He] would tear the papers up and throw them away."[60]

Mirza Habib also writes about 'Abdu'l-Bahá's pleasant and sweet temperament:

> Despite all the troubles, difficulties, injuries, imprisonment, opposition, hostilities, and threats that surrounded every instant of His life, which gave no opportunity for a moment's respite, 'Abdu'l-Bahá was never fatigued or depressed and was never heard to complain or show remorse. He was always happy and jubilant in the midst of difficulties and tribulations. Unperturbed by the onrush of obstacles, [He] would share humorous anecdotes to lighten the moment. In fact, during such times, He would engage in trimming flowerbeds, renovating the Shrine of Bahá'u'lláh and other Bahá'í Holy Places, and even organizing weddings and feasts. He was never saddened or depressed, except when the violators of the Covenant had caused the betrayal of a believer or news of disunity among the friends was received.[61]

Mirza Habib writes with unique sharp-sightedness about 'Abdu'l-Bahá's habits:

> 'Abdu'l-Bahá's eating habits were most amazing and noteworthy. Often at the dinner table, holding a pitcher of water and speaking, He would serve food and assure the comfort of His guests. He would eat only after everyone had dined. His bites were very small, less than the size of an almond, and would be chewed

very well. He ate extremely slowly, did not like meat, nor cared very much for fruits, but occasionally took a tangerine or a sweet lemon. Most of the time His food was bread, milk, cheese, and raw vegetables, particularly mint, tarragon and sweet basil. Altogether, He ate little and drank very hot tea, which toward the end of His life was changed to herbal tea.[62] He ate and slept little.[63]

Moayyad writes about 'Abdu'l-Bahá, that celestial personage and His love for nature:

> Early this morning, 'Abdu'l-Bahá went to the Jamí'al-Jazzár [Mosque of Jazzár], and from there, proceeded directly to the Shrine of Bahá'u'lláh. Soon thereafter, His carriage returned, and the honored Isfandiyár, the carriage driver, informed us of the joyous news that we had been summoned [to Bahjí]. We immediately proceeded to the shrine of Bahá'u'lláh.

> It was in the flower gardens around the Shrine that the beauty of the Master illumined our eyes. Indeed, the beauty of the Adored One had robbed the flowers of their charm! That luminous Person, with His celestial traits, clothed in completely white garments with a white headdress, . . . stood out amidst the multitude of jasmine and multicolored flowers.

> As He paced, we entered His presence,

bowed down, and were warmly greeted. My God, what immense bounty this is! Are we asleep or conscious, intoxicated or sober? How truly exalted are the divine favors bestowed so graciously upon us! How magnificent the feast spread before us and how profound is such delight! How truly fortunate we are![64]

The Master's care and mercy towards the pilgrims, whether rich or poor, are noted as follows:

Day and night the pilgrims were in the utmost ecstasy and rapture, their spirits soaring to the Supreme Concourse, thoroughly oblivious to worldly concerns and such mundane things as food. Rich and poor were one and the same. All were profoundly devoted to the Beloved and adored His heavenly, moon-brilliant Countenance. Neither superiority nor inferiority existed among the pilgrims. Rich or poor, we all sat at the same table, enjoyed the same food and drank from the same chalice of love. "How magnificent is that assemblage of love where the deprived sits equal to the king!"

To cheer the friends, His Holiness 'Abdu'l-Bahá often came and joined us in meals. After inspecting the kitchen and the situation of the pilgrims, 'Abdu'l-Bahá would provide the necessary instructions for improvements.[65]

Dr. Moayyad describes the Master's caring attitude towards children and especially the importance of teaching calligraphy in this way:

> Each Friday morning, Bahá'í children attained the presence of 'Abdu'l-Bahá and presented their weekly studies and exercise. He reviewed and corrected most and gave each student a prize. The children did their work and nasta'líq calligraphy, taught by Mishkín-Qalam and, because of him, all Bahá'í students had exquisite handwriting. This pattern in the Holy Land is now the model for all Bahá'í children's classes.[66]

The spiritual relationship between the Most Great Branch ['Abdu'l-Bahá] and His father [Bahá'u'lláh] was like that of worshipper and the worshipped, or a lover and his beloved.[67] The following incident that took place in Bahjí on October 30, 1914, testifies to this dynamic:

> We spent our days and nights in this pilgrim house under the shadow of the Shrine of Bahá'u'lláh and in the proximity of the room where the Master resided and rested, and where we benefited from His divine favors. There was only a thin wall between our room and the Master's. Every night, we would hear the murmur of His prayers and the melody of His supplications.
>
> Twice a day, morning and the afternoon, we would visit the Shrine of Bahá'u'lláh. The

Master would chant the Tablet of Visitation with such reverence, humility, and longing that all who were present would be profoundly moved. May my life be a sacrifice for the Master! May it be a ransom to this peerless Servant! He teaches us the lessons of servitude and modesty, sets the example of humility and altruism, instructs selflessness and self-annihilation, proclaims the ways of meekness and consecration, and embodies the meaning of certitude and worship. He has no desire for praise and recognition, and only seeks to manifest the true nature of obedience and love-physically and spiritually, outwardly and inwardly—as an expression of His very essence. He lived in utter love and absolute adoration of the Blessed Beauty. Truly, the Ancient Beauty was well served in such a magnificent Son and such a glorious Father![68] That is, the Father was to be praised and recognized for such a Son, and the Son was befitting and worthy of the trust of such a Father! Father and Son are connected by one sanctified Spirit, and may my soul be a sacrifice unto Both![69]

At this point a different anecdote is presented which demonstrates 'Abdu'l-Bahá's unconditional love and favor to the lovers of the Blessed Beauty [Bahá'u'lláh], and also His servitude and lowliness towards Him. In the second year of his medical studies, Habib Moayyad was feeling weak and miserable because of financial difficulties and tremendous preoccupation with his studies. He sent a letter to the Master, which he describes thus:

> During my hours of solitude, I supplicated 'Abdu'l-Bahá in my heart and fervently besought His assistance. With tearful eyes and soul on fire, I would compose supplications and submit them unto His august and sanctified presence. Indeed, it was a strange year. From every direction, troubles and difficulties beset me and I was overwhelmed by their stress and gravity. Every time a letter arrived from my father, it was filled with grievous and most unhappy tidings and lamentations. He informed me of the plunder of our house by the Sáláru'd-Dawlih and many other troubles that unceasingly surrounded them [his family].[70] My nerves were fatigued, my body weak, and my spirit depressed. All strength was drained from my being.
>
> Below is a section that I recall from a poetic missive [Hold Thou My Hand, 'Abdu'l-Bahá (dastam begir 'Abdu'l-Bahá in Persian)] that I composed at that time, which to some degree conveyed the intensity of the tribulations and the fire of misery, pain, depression, and paralysis that had engulfed me, and yet I had to advance in my studies and continue with life's struggles:

O Hadrat-i 'Abdu'l-Bahá,
   O Center of the Covenant of Bahá,
O Builder of the House of God,
   Hold Thou my hand, 'Abdu'l-Bahá,
'Abdu'l-Bahá, have mercy on me,
   Sacrifice my life for Thee,
Sacrifice it for Thy locks,
   Hold Thou my hand, 'Abdu'l-Bahá,
'Abdu'l-Bahá, Thou art aware,
   Thou art life-taker and life-giver,
Thou art the guide of every wayward,
   Hold Thou my hand, 'Abdu'l-Bahá,
'Abdu'l-Bahá, I am wretched,
   I have no hope and am lost,
Like a babe in the cradle.
   Hold Thou my hand, 'Abdu'l-Bahá,
O Jehovah, resplendent Lord,
   Have mercy on this ill one,
O promise of the tribe of Abraham,
   Hold Thou my hand, 'Abdu'l-Bahá.[71]

Moayyad then received two Tablets from 'Abdu'l-Bahá that were filled with affection. He continues:

In response to my supplication, a Tablet was revealed that was the cure of all my ills. All my sorrow and melancholy vanished completely. I forgot every pain that had ever afflicted me, and with new vigor and infinite enthusiasm I resumed my studies and activities. A few days later, yet another Tablet was received that redoubled my joy and brought me an even larger measure of delight and felicity.[72]

In yet another Tablet, 'Abdu'l-Bahá acknowledges the sweet and fluent expressions of Moayyad, whom he calls a friend steadfast in the Covenant. He states, however, that Moayyad's talent in praise and supplication must be used in worship and honoring of the Greatest Name, meaning Bahá'u'lláh. Considering Himself a drop and Bahá'u'lláh the ocean, 'Abdu'l-Bahá states that when the ocean is praised, the drop is included.[73]

A story of the awe-inspiring insight and knowledge of the Great Mystery of God regarding the future told by Bushrui has been presented.[74] Here we share yet another example of His foresight and vision from the memoirs of Moayyad:

> On one occasion, when 'Abdu'l-Bahá was strolling in the gardens [near the Shrine of the Báb] His eyes were focused upon the sea and the city of 'Akká for some time. After a few moments of silence, He said, "I have seen many places abroad, but nowhere has the fresh air and the beautiful scenery of the Shrine of the Báb. Ere long this mountain will become habitable. Many fine buildings will be built on it. The Shrine of the Báb will be constructed in the most exquisite fashion and will appear with the utmost beauty and magnificence. Terraces will be built from the bottom of the mountain to the top, nine terraces from the bottom to the Shrine and nine terraces from the Shrine to the summit. Gardens with colourful flowers will be laid down on all

these terraces. A single street lined with flower beds will link the seafront to the Shrine. Pilgrims who arrive by ship will be able to see the dome of the Shrine from a long distance out at sea. The kings of the earth, bare-headed, and the queens, will walk up the street of the Shrine carrying bouquets of flowers. With bowed heads they will arrive as pilgrims, and prostrate themselves at the sacred threshold."[75]

Dr. Moayyad, after having been a practicing physician for a while, received an exceptional honor, the account of which he preserved in his memoirs. This anecdote is another witness to the Beloved's knowledge and awareness of the deeds and doings of the future. He writes:

> There was a particular wish that was always present in my thoughts, but I would not be presumptuous enough to speak of it. I always wanted to perform a physical examination of 'Abdu'l-Bahá and know the details of His condition. I wanted to closely examine His internal organs [His internal health], to determine the state of each of the principal bodily systems at His age, and establish which one, if any, was not functioning properly and if He suffered from any ailment. In short, this was my long cherished desire and this thought never left me.
>
> Indeed, day-by-day, it [this yearning] grew

stronger and enveloped my thoughts. However, every time I thought of actually suggesting this idea to the Master, a great turmoil would overwhelm me - my heart would beat loudly, I would gasp for breath, my throat would become dry, and my whole being would shake. Therefore, I would remain silent and not speak of this idea. It was like this for a while, but this wish never left me.

One day without any prior discussion, 'Abdu'l-Bahá said, "Mirzá Habíb, God wanted your labor not to go to waste and, therefore, enabled you to serve the divine friends. And now you remedy their ills. Come remedy Me as well. I want you to give Me a thorough physical examination. You cannot just cure all others except Me!"

I realized that in that instant my long cherished hope had materialized and my prayers had been answered. I was so thrilled that I was shaking, my heart was palpitating, and my tongue was tied. Nevertheless, I began the examination.

'Abdu'l-Bahá removed His clothes and shirt and, with the utmost care, I examined every organ and vital part from the tip of His head to his toes.[76]

No sign of sickness or illness was found, and Dr. Moayyad continued:

In short, I found nothing abnormal in my

examination and reported the result to
'Abdu'l-Bahá, saying, "I did not note anything
that could be a cause of illness." He replied,
"When the doctors in Europe examined Me,
they too did not find anything wrong.[77] My
fever is a fever of the nerves. It is not related
to any bodily organs. My nerves are tired,
since waves of tribulations do not cease to
waft over Me. However, through the bounties
and favors of the Blessed Beauty, My spirit is
refreshed and cheered."

Dr. Moayyad narrates the story of the first Naw-Rúz after
the end of World War I which was celebrated with particular
pleasure. He speaks of the Master's detachment and humility
in this manner:

All the believers in Abu Sinan, 'Akká,
Haifa, the Gardens and Bahjí were present,
numbering about seventy men and
undoubtedly the same number of women.
What a magnificent day and delightful
morning![78] All heavenly bounties were
arrayed: the grace of beholding the visage of
the Beloved, the visit to the Shrine of
Bahá'u'lláh, meeting the friends, the colorful
and vivifying flowers, the luscious fruits, the
sweetmeats, confections, tea, and two cooked
lambs that had been purchased on the Master's
instructions. Early in the morning 'Abdu'l-
Bahá came from 'Akká to Bahjí and in the
kitchen prepared food for the friends.

> Consider how He teaches humility, service, and sacrifice to his sinful servants who have not inhaled the perfume of detachment and how the clouds of His bounties shower down the rain of grace, though naught save motes and specks grow in the soil of our hearts![79]

A few days before dismissing Dr. Moayyad from the Holy Land, the Master summoned him and told him thus:

> I have an instruction for thee which thou shouldst communicate everywhere. That command and instruction is this: that My Name, designation and title, nay my reality, my essential being and nature is Servitude of Bahá, 'Abdu'l-Bahá. No one should utter a word of my description other than this. All letters addressed to Me should be preceded by this invocation, namely: O 'Abdu'l-Bahá. After that preface then ask of Me whatever ye wish expressing all your desire and purpose. I entreat ye all to accept this so that all may arise in the servitude of the Blessed Beauty [Bahá'u'lláh] so that all hearts may become illumined with the bounties of servitude and all souls may obtain full grace of servitude to that Divine Beauty.[80]

There are numerous stories of the attributes of 'Abdu'l-Bahá by Dr. Moayyad, who was enamored of His love.

Shrine of the Báb in 1909 on Mount Carmel during
the time of 'Abdu'l-Bahá

Shrine of the Báb today

Visit of 'Abdu'l-Bahá to the West

'Abdu'l-Bahá, who was liberated from his forty-year confinement in the prison city of 'Akká by the Young Turks revolution in 1908, set sail for Egypt in 1910. His journeys to the West were a series of trips that He undertook starting at age 67 from Egypt from 1911 to 1913. He traveled in the twilight of His years and on the eve of World War I to promulgate universal peace, a central teaching of this new religion. The arrival of 'Abdu'l-Bahá in the West would be one of the most important experiences of His devotees' lives.

His first journey to the West started in August 1911 when he left for France, took a short visit to Switzerland and then visited Britain and revisited France, after which he returned to Egypt in December. His second journey to the West was to North America. He arrived in New York on April 11, 1912, and traveled coast-to-coast by train in the United States, visiting fifty cities and towns. During His travels, 'Abdu'l-

Bahá gave talks at universities and private societies, and in churches, synagogues, and the homes of Bahá'ís. He also visited Montreal, Canada, home of May and Sutherland Maxwell, who were early champions of the Faith. He then sailed for Liverpool, England, and gave talks there and in Bristol, Edinburgh, London, and Oxford. He left London for Paris on January 21, 1913, and from there He went to Germany, Hungary, and Austria, finally returning to Paris. His return to Egypt was in June 1913.[81]

Throughout these trips 'Abdu'l-Bahá proclaimed the message of the oneness of humanity, the need for social justice, and many other teachings of Bahá'u'lláh in small and large gatherings in churches, universities, labor union meetings, and gatherings with intellectuals and government officials. He also gave many interviews with newspaper reporters. He attracted large audiences of people from all walks of life who were eager to hear His words. 'Abdu'l-Bahá spoke as easily with the leaders of thought, governmental and church officials, as with the humble workman, the forgotten poor, and the political radical. It is recorded that "His reputation as a saintly figure endowed with innate wisdom quickly grew, and was widely reported in the press."[82]

Often individuals were overwhelmed by the presence of 'Abdu'l-Bahá.[83] These encounters were life-altering for many of those who met Him because he touched the depths of their souls and awakened them spiritually. For many who met 'Abdu'l-Bahá during His trips to the West, the experience may not have "conveyed more than a contact with personified dignity, beauty, wisdom, and selflessness, and so led them, at least, to higher attitudes of thought and life"; however, for hundreds of others "that was the door to [an] undreamed-of-world, to a new, a boundless, [and] an eternal life."[84]

Many Western believers as well as non-Bahá'í individuals were privileged to meet 'Abdu'l-Bahá and to partake of the sweetness of his character during His two journeys to Europe and North America. Of the many people who later wrote down their memories of meeting 'Abdu'l-Bahá, excerpts from the memoirs of two enkindled souls from the West are selected for this compilation—Lady Blomfield, 'Abdu'l-Bahá's hostess in London, and Howard Colby Ives, a clergyman who met 'Abdu'l-Bahá during His visit to New York.

The memoirs of these two faithful believers are among the finest accounts of 'Abdu'l-Bahá's travels and His meetings with people in the West, narratives that give the reader insight into 'Abdu'l-Bahá's way of "teaching souls."[85] These memoirs of Lady Blomfield and Ives are not only sweet and charming, but are educational and inspiring as well.

'Abdu'l-Bahá in Great Britain, circa 1911

'Abdu'l-Bahá in America, circa 1912

Lady Sara Blomfield

Lady Blomfield was born Sara Louisa Ryan in Ireland in 1859.[86] Her father was Irish Catholic, her mother English Protestant. Her childhood was spent in an environment of religious conflict; this experience deeply affected her and caused her to quest for spiritual truth. She spent her adult life in London. Sara became Lady Blomfield when her husband, architect Arthur Blomfield, was knighted by Queen Victoria.[87] She became an accomplished writer and humanitarian. Lady Blomfield accepted the Bahá'í teachings in 1907 at the age of 48 and this marked the turning point in her lifelong search for divine truth. Her embrace of Bahá'í principles increased her desire to see justice and equality established in the world. She became involved in philanthropic activities in service to the oppressed and needy. Her humanitarian activities include her work with the League of Nations.[88]

During 'Abdu'l-Bahá's visit to Paris in 1911, she took notes of His public talks and these were used in preparing the book called *Paris Talks*.[89] She also welcomed the Master during His first visit to London in 1911 by hosting Him at her home at 97 Cadogan Gardens. At the outbreak of World War I, she was living in Switzerland but left for Paris and volunteered with the French Red Cross. She returned to London in 1915 where she helped several hospitals and also kept in touch with 'Abdu'l-Bahá in Haifa. She followed His recommendation and intensified her humanitarian and social activities, in particular those concerned with the rights of women and children. 'Abdu'l-Bahá gave her the name "Sitárih Khánum."[90]

After the passing of the Master in 1921, Lady Blomfield traveled to Haifa to be with His family. She was not only considered a friend but as a dear "family member."[91] During this stay, she interviewed members of the Holy Family and wrote extensive notes on them. Those records, together with her accounts of the days of 'Abdu'l-Bahá's visit to London, comprised the contents of her book *The Chosen Highway*.[92] This work, finished on the eve of her death, was a great achievement.[93] Lady Blomfield, a distinguished early Bahá'í, passed away peacefully at age 80 on the last day of the year 1939.

Memories of Lady Sara Blomfield

When Lady Blomfield heard the news that 'Abdu'l-Bahá
had been released from forty years of imprisonment and that
He intended to visit the West, she expressed her ecstatic
feelings as follows:

> The beloved Prisoner was free! Free to
> obey the charge laid upon Him by Bahá'u'lláh
> to go forth into all the world to carry the
> message of the Renewal of Peace and Unity,
> of Joy and Service.
>
> We waited and wondered whether it was to
> be our privilege to see Him. Would it be given
> to us to hear the teaching of Bahá'u'lláh from
> 'Abdu'l-Bahá Himself?
>
> Should we travel to Egypt, or would He
> come to Europe? If He were to come to
> London, where would be the roof to shelter
> Him? We who had quietly prepared our home
> in the hope that He Might deign to sojourn

there awhile, sent the invitation. Soon a
telegram came: "Abdu'l-Bahá arriving in
London 8th September (1911). Can Lady
Blomfield receive Him?"

And now at last 'Abdu'l-Bahá was coming
into the western world, even to us in London.

He arrived, and who shall picture Him? He
came with hands outstretched.[94]

As soon as 'Abdu'l-Bahá arrived, He expressed immense
joy and love and said:

"I am very much pleased with you all.
Your love has drawn me to London. I waited
forty years in prison to bring the Message to
you. Are you pleased to receive such a
guest?"[95]

Lady Blomfield continues:

I think our souls must have answered, for I
am not conscious that anyone uttered an
audible word.[96]

She then notes His tender emotions and sense of
appreciation:

The Master's custom was to receive the
visitors by twos or threes, or individually,
during the early hours of the morning. Then,
about nine o'clock, He would come into the
dining room whilst we were at breakfast to
greet us. "Are you well? Did you sleep well?"

We tried to prevail upon Him to take some

breakfast with us (we were always concerned that he ate so very little). At last one day He said He would like a little soup—then we had it brought in every morning. He smiled and said: "To please you I will take it. Thank you, you are very kind." Then to the servitor who offered it to Him: "I give too great trouble," He said.

In a few minutes He would go to His room, where He would resume the chanting of prayers and dictating of Tablets in reply to the vast number of letters which incessantly arrived.

Visitors having gradually gathered in the drawing-room, 'Abdu'l-Bahá would come to us, pausing just inside the door, smiling round at the guests with a look of joyous sympathy which seemed to enfold each and all who were present; they rose simultaneously, as though the kingship of this Messenger were recognized by an inner perception.

"How are you? My hope is that you are well. Are you happy?"

Speaking so to us, He would pass through our midst to His usual chair. Then He would talk rather with us than to us; so did He reply to unspoken questions, causing wonderment in those who were waiting to ask them—weaving the whole into a beautiful address, in the atmosphere of which all problems and pain and care and doubt and sorrow would melt away, leaving only happiness and peace.

The power of Divine Love we felt to be incarnated in Him, Whom we called "the Master."[97]

Lady Blomfield writes about the Master's consideration for the poor and needy members of the community in this way:

After His first dinner with us He said: "The food was delicious and the fruit and flowers were lovely, but would that we could share some of the courses with those poor and hungry people who have not even one." What a lesson to the guests present![98]

In another story, she recalls:

A Persian friend arrived who had passed through Ishqábád. He presented a cotton handkerchief to 'Abdu'l-Bahá, who untied it, and saw therein a piece of dry black bread, and a shriveled apple.

The friend exclaimed: "A poor Bahá'í workman came to me and said: 'I hear thou goest into the presence of our Beloved. Nothing have I to send, but this my dinner. I pray thee offer it to Him with my loving devotion.'" 'Abdu'l-Bahá spread the poor handkerchief before Him, leaving His own luncheon untouched. He ate of the workman's dinner, broke pieces off the bread, and handed them to the assembled guests, saying: "Eat with me of this gift of humble love."[99]

She continues:

> Of the guests who remained to lunch or dinner, the Master would often hold out His hand to the humblest or most diffident, lead them into the dining-room, seat him or her at His right hand, smile and talk until all embarrassment had passed away, and the guest felt as though all uneasiness had changed into the atmosphere of a calm and happy home.[100]

Magnanimity of character was another of His attributes. Lady Blomfield writes:

> One striking fact was that 'Abdu'l-Bahá never asked for donations, and even refused to accept money or any costly gifts that were offered to Him.
>
> One day in my presence a lady said to Him: "I have here a check from a friend, who begs its acceptance to buy a good motor-car for your work in England and Europe."
>
> The Master replied: "I accept with grateful thanks the gift of your friend." He took the cheque into both His hands, as though blessing it, and said "I return it to be used for gifts to the poor."
>
> "We have never seen the like before. Surely such deeds are very rare," it was whispered amongst the friends.[101]

Another story shows His loving kindness and His sense of joy and happiness in seeing others happy. Lady Blomfield describes:

> His desire that everyone should be happy showed itself in many ways. "Are you well? Are you happy?" he always asked.
>
> One day the sound of peals of laughter came from the direction of the kitchen. The Master went quickly to the cheery party.
>
> "I am very much pleased that you are so happy. Tell me, why are you laughing?"
>
> It appeared that the Persian servant had remarked, "In the East women wear veils and do all the work," to which our English housekeeper had replied: "In the West women don't wear veils, and take good care that the men do at least some of the work. You had better get on with cleaning that silver."
>
> The Master was delighted, laughed heartily, and gave each of them a small gold coin, "for being happy."[102]

The next account illustrates how His innate spiritual power energized His beloved being. Lady Blomfield writes:

> One day after a meeting when, as usual, many people had crowded round Him, 'Abdu'l-Bahá arrived home very tired. We were sad at heart that He should be so fatigued, and bewailed the many steps to be ascended to the flat. Suddenly, to our amazement, the Master ran up the stairs to the

top very quickly without stopping.

He looked down at us as we walked up after Him, saying with a bright smile, from which all traces of fatigue had vanished: "You are all very old! I am very young!"

Seeing me full of wonder, 'Abdu'l-Bahá said: "Through the power of Bahá'u'lláh all things can be done. I have just used that power."

That was the only time we had ever seen Him use that power for Himself, and I feel that He did so then to cheer and comfort us, as we were really sad concerning His fatigue.

Might it not also have been to show us an example of the great Reserve of Divine Force always available for those of us who are working in various ways in the "Path of the Love of God and of Mankind?" A celestial strength which reinforces us when our human strength fails.[103]

One night, while returning from a gathering and driving through the streets of London, 'Abdu'l-Bahá uttered the following words about true freedom. Lady Blomfield records:

Rows of shining lamps beneath the trees, stretching as far as our eyes could see in the distance, made that part of London into a glowing fairyland.

"I am very much pleased with this scene. Light is good, most good. There was much darkness in the prison at 'Akká," said the

Master.

Our hearts were sad as we thought on those somber years within that dismal fortress, where the only light was in the indomitable spirit of the Master Himself! When we said: "We are glad, oh! so full of gladness that you are free." He said: "Freedom is not a matter of place, but of condition. I was happy in that prison; for those days were passed in the path of service.... Therefore was I full of happiness all through that prison time. When one is released from the prison of self; that is indeed freedom! For self is the greatest prison."[104]

'Abdu'l-Bahá's compassionate love was for all, treating everyone as members of His family. Let us consider this memory of Lady Blomfield:

One day, whilst I was driving with Mrs. Cropper and the Master, she said: "Master, are you not longing to be back at Haifa with your beloved family?" He smiled and said: "I wish you to understand that you are both as truly my dear daughters, as beloved by me, as are those of whom you speak."

Our hearts thrilled with joy and awe as He spoke. "How can we serve to be even a little worthy of so high an honor?[105]

Sitárih Khánum witnessed 'Abdu'l-Bahá's trust and faith in the Will of God:

One day, I received a disquieting letter: "It

would be well to warn 'Abdu'l-Bahá that it might be dangerous for Him to visit a certain country, for which I understand He proposes to set forth in the near future."

Having regard to the sincere friendship of the writer, and knowing that sources of reliable information were available to him, this warning obviously could not be ignored. Therefore, as requested, I laid the matter before the Master.

To my amazement, He smiled and said impressively: "My daughter, have you not yet realized that never, in my life, have I been for one day out of danger, and that I should rejoice to leave this world and go to my Father?"

"Oh, Master! We do not wish that you should go from us in that manner." I was overcome with sorrow and terror.

"Be not troubled," said 'Abdu'l-Bahá. "These enemies have no power over my life, but that which is given them from on High. If my Beloved God so willed that my life-blood should be sacrificed in His path, it would be a glorious day, devoutly wished for by me."

Therefore the friends surrounding the much-loved Master were comforted, and their faith so strengthened, that when a sinister-looking man came up to a group who were walking in the gardens and threateningly said: "Are you not yet sufficiently warned. Not only is there danger for 'Abdu'l-Bahá, but also for you who are with Him," the friends were unperturbed, one of them replying calmly: "The power that protects the Master protects also His other servants. Therefore we have no fear."[106]

This section ends with a quote from Lady Blomfield as 'Abdu'l-Bahá's stay in London came to closure and grief was brought to the hearts of those who had met Him:

> 'Abdu'l-Bahá's sojourn in London was ended. We stood bereft of His presence.
>
> Discarding preconceived ideas, a new consciousness seemed to awaken when in His presence.
>
> Some of the minds, though as yet so finite, reached out to recognition of the Light of the great Manifestation, now being diffused by 'Abdu'l-Bahá on all Humanity. To us He was impregnated with that Light, "as a vesture wrapped about him, like a garment round him thrown."
>
> Small wonder that we mortals were overwhelmed with awe, as we drew near to the heavenly Messenger of that Immortal Spirit of Truth and Light, which had come to save the children of men from chaotic destruction.
>
> Would humanity awaken? Or would they continue to sleep "unaware"?[107]

Howard Colby Ives

Howard Colby Ives was born in Brooklyn, New York, in 1867 and lost his father while young. At age 35, he entered a Unitarian theological school in Pennsylvania and graduated three years later. He was 46 years old in 1912 when met 'Abdu'l-Bahá in New York. He spent many hours in the company of the Master and declared his faith in Bahá'u'lláh three months after that first visit.

In his spiritual autobiography *Portals to Freedom*, Ives divides his life distinctly into two parts—the 46 years before he met 'Abdu'l-Bahá, which he compares to the experience of a child of ten! And the second phase, which began when 'Abdu'l-Bahá came to New York in April 1912, an event he refers to as "another birth."[108]

Ives wrote at length about his impressions of his first meeting with 'Abdu'l-Bahá, including His "majestic" behavior, His gentleness, and His love. The Master had singled him out, a minister from New Jersey, from among the crowds of people that had come to meet him! Of the interview that followed, Ives said this: "He looked at me! It seemed as though never before had anyone seen me." This is how he ends this section in his book:

> He ['Abdu'l-Bahá] kissed both my cheeks;
> He put his hands on my shoulder and led me
> toward the door. That is all. But life has never
> been quite the same since.[109]

Ives later wrote:

> Indeed to have seen Him was enough
> providing that the spark ignited in the soul was
> fanned to flame by meditation and selfless
> prayer. Never can I be thankful enough that I
> became ignited with this Flame. ... I began to
> say a little hymn to myself: "If every drop of
> my blood had a million tongues and every
> tongue sang praises throughout eternity,
> sufficient thanksgiving could not be
> uttered."[110]

Ives ceased his Christian ministerial work to become what 'Abdu'l-Bahá honored him as describing a "Minister of the Temple of the Kingdom."[111] By studying the Bahá'í Writings, he became highly respected for his knowledge of the Bahá'í Faith. In 1919 Ives married a devoted Bahá'í, Mabel Rice-Wray, who was "aflame with the same spirit of renunciation and service."[112] This marriage was like "the juncture of two swift running streams: from the moment of that union, the [two] streams became a river."[113] They sold or gave away all their possessions the year after their marriage and started the odyssey of serving their faith. They traveled the rest of their lives giving lectures, seminars, classes, and public talks on the Bahá'í Faith. In a letter to his daughter, Ives said:

> Abdu'l-Bahá's words "Homeless and without rest" ring in my ears, when He is describing the attributes of the Apostles of Bahá'u'lláh. Rest assured that God does not take away an earthly home without providing a heavenly one right here on earth if we accept His will with radiant acquiescence.

Howard Colby Ives passed away in 1941 at the age of 74 and his soul undoubtedly soared to his beloved Master.

Memories of Howard Colby Ives

This section begins with an illustration of 'Abdu'l-Bahá's patience and acceptance of others. A few days after Ives' first meeting with 'Abdu'l-Bahá in the spring of 1912, he saw Him again at another event. On that day, the Master was speaking of an aspect of Christian doctrine, and His interpretation of the words of Christ was quite different from the accepted one. Ives could not restrain an expression of remonstrance. He writes:

> I remember speaking with some heat: "How is it possible to be so sure?" I asked. "No one can say with certainty what Jesus meant after all these centuries of misinterpretation and strife." He intimated that it was quite possible.
>
> It is indicative of my spiritual turmoil and my blindness to His station that instead of His serenity and tone of authority impressing me

as warranted it drove me to actual impatience. "That, I cannot believe," I exclaimed.

I shall never forget the glance of outraged dignity the interpreter cast upon me. It was as though he would say: "Who are you to contradict or even to question 'Abdu'l-Bahá!"

But not so did 'Abdu'l-Bahá look at me. How I thank God that it was not! He looked at me a long moment before He spoke. His calm beautiful eyes searched my soul with such love and understanding that all my momentary heat evaporated. He smiled as winningly as a lover smiles upon his beloved, and the arms of His spirit seemed to embrace me as He said softly that I should try my way and He would try His.

It was as though a cool hand had been laid upon a fevered brow; as though a cup of nectar had been held to parched lips; as though a key had unlocked my hard-bolted, crusted and rusted heart. The tears started and my voice trembled, "I am sorry," I murmured.[114]

Ives describes the amazing method of teaching used by 'Abdu'l-Bahá:

In all of my many opportunities of meeting, of listening to and talking with 'Abdu'l-Bahá, I was impressed, and constantly more deeply impressed, with His method of teaching souls. That is the word. He did not attempt to reach the mind alone. He sought the soul, the reality of every one He met. Oh, He could be logical, even scientific in His presentation of an argument, as He demonstrated constantly in the many addresses I have heard Him give and the many more I have read. But it was not the logic of the schoolman, not the science of the class room. His lightest word, His slightest association with the soul was shot through with an illuminating radiance which lifted the hearer to a higher plane of consciousness. Our hearts burned within us when He spoke. And He never argued, of course. Nor did He press a point. He left one free.

There was never an assumption of authority; rather He was ever the personification of humility. He taught "as if offering a gift to a king." He never told me what I should do, beyond suggesting that what I was doing was right. Nor did He ever tell me what I should believe. He made Truth and Love so beautiful and royal that the heart perforce did reverence. He showed me by His voice, manner, bearing, smile, how I should *be*, knowing that out of the pure soil of being the good fruit of deeds and words would surely spring.

There was a strange, awe-inspiring mingling of humility and majesty, relaxation and power in His slightest word or gesture which made me long to understanding its source. What made Him so different, so immeasurably superior to any other man I had ever met?[115]

'Abdu'l-Bahá had a busy schedule during His stay in New York in 1912. This story shows the level of His divine energy and power:

> Even His physical condition was reinforced constantly by this Divine Power. On one occasion after a particularly exhausting day He was returning late at night from a gathering at which He had spoken with much energy and effectiveness. In the automobile he showed great weariness. He relaxed and gradually sank into almost a comatose condition. The friends who were with Him were greatly alarmed. On arriving at their destination, He had to be almost carried into the house and to His room. Within fifteen minutes, while the friends were gathered in great anxiety in the lower rooms, His voice was heard resounding with even more than its usual energy and power calling for His secretary, and He appeared at the top of the stairs His usual dominant, smiling, forceful self.[116]

In regard to His generosity and magnanimity, Ives writes:

> . . . 'Abdu'l-Bahá had no contract (no obligation) other than the Covenant of selfless Servitude made with Bahá'u'lláh in the sanctuary of His heart, and, furthermore, so far from demanding or expecting any financial regard, He consistently refused the slightest

remuneration, and even when entertained by solicitous and generous hosts He was punctilious in seeing to it that gifts to both host and servants of the household far outweighed what He received. When He stayed at hotels his "tips" to servants who waited on Him were often so generous as to excite astonishment. But even this does not all cover what He gave. In several instances that have come to my personal knowledge, His spiritual influence upon chambermaids and porters was such that one of them said to one of those accompanying the Master: "This is sacred money. I shall never spend it upon myself."[117]

'Abdu'l-Bahá was the ultimate symbol of humility and consideration, demonstrated clearly as follows:

His whole bearing was ever that of humility and gentle deference. Yet in every home He entered he was the host, in every gathering the center, in every discussion the arbiter, to every problem the answer.

Nor was it so because He wished or willed it so to be. On the contrary, when He was asked to act as honorary chairman of the New York Bahá'í Assembly, . . . He calmly and decisively replied that "Abdu'l-Bahá is a servant."

Nevertheless one could not be in His presence more than a few moments without realizing that His every act, tone, gesture, word was so imbued with wisdom, courage and tranquil certitude, combined with such humble consideration of His interlocutor, that conclusive Truth was conveyed to every beholder and listener.[118]

'Abdu'l-Bahá's all-embracing love and promotions of equality were shown in simple ways. The following tells about the visit of about twenty-five boys who were invited to meet with 'Abdu'l-Bahá:

'Abdu'l-Bahá was standing at the door and He greeted each boy as he came in, sometimes with a handclasp, sometimes with an arm around a shoulder, but always with such smiles and laughter it almost seemed that He was a boy with them. Certainly there was no suggestion of stillness on their part, or awkwardness in their unaccustomed surroundings. Among the last to enter the room was a colored lad of about thirteen years. He was quite dark and, being the only boy of his race among them, he evidently feared that he might not be welcome. When 'Abdu'l-Bahá saw him, His face lighted up with a heavenly smile. He raised His hand with a gesture of princely welcome and exclaimed in a loud voice so that none could fail to hear that there was a black rose.

The room fell into instant silence. The black face became illumined with a happiness and love hardly of this world. The other boys looked at him with new eyes. I venture to say that he had been called a black- many things, but never before a black rose. . . . To the few friends in the room the scene brought visions of a new world in which every soul would be recognized and treated as a child of God.[119]

'Abdu'l-Bahá spoke in Persian and the interpreter translated. His penetrating utterance was such that one was entranced and understood inwardly even before the interpreter opened his mouth. Ives experienced this marvel as follows:

In spite of the fact that the language was Persian, and so, of course, unfamiliar to me, the impression I received was that of understanding.

So vivid was this that the interpreter's translation came as a shock. What need to translate language addressed to the spirit? A flash of comprehension came to me. Perhaps here was the explanation of the incident recorded of that far-off Day of Pentecost when each listener to the word of the disciples heard his own tongue.

There is a story told of an illiterate miner who made a long journey on foot to meet 'Abdu'l-Bahá when He was in San Francisco, which further illustrates the same spiritual phenomenon. He attended a meeting at which 'Abdu'l-Bahá spoke. He seemed enthralled as the measured, bell-like tones fell from the

Master's lips. When the interpreter took up the passage in English this miner started as if awakening. "Why does that man interrupt?" he whispered. Then again 'Abdu'l-Bahá spoke, and again the visitor was lost in attention. Again the interpreter translated as the speaker paused. At this the miner's indignation was aroused. "Why do they let that man interrupt? He should be put out."

"He is the official interpreter," one sitting beside him explained. "He translates the Persian into English."

"Was He speaking in Persian?" was the naïve answer, "Why anyone could understand that."[120]

Ives writes about the Master's silence in this way:

Another characteristic always apparent was His silence. In the world of social and intellectual intercourse to which I was accustomed, silence was almost unforgivable . . . . How differently 'Abdu'l-Bahá met the questioner, the conversationalist, and the occasion: To the questioner He responded first with silence - an outward silence. His encouragement always was that the other should speak and He listen. There was never that eager tenseness, that restlessness so often met showing most plainly that the listener has the pat answer ready the moment he should have a chance to utter it.

I have heard certain people described as "good listeners," but never had I imagined such a "listener" as 'Abdu'l-Bahá. It was more than a sympathetic absorption of what the ear received. It was as though the two individualities became one, as if He so closely identified Himself with the one speaking that merging of spirits occurred which made a verbal response almost unnecessary, superfluous.[121]

After listening to a talk by 'Abdu'l-Bahá in a church, Ives remembers:

What His subject was I do not recall, nor does a single word of His address remain with me. My memory is all of the quiet New England church, the crowded pews, and 'Abdu'l-Bahá on the platform. His cream-colored robe, His white hair and beard, His radiant smile and courteous demeanor. And His gestures! Never a dogmatic downward stroke of the hand, never an upraised warning finger, never the assumption of teacher to the taught. But always the encouraging upward swing of hands, as though He would actually lift us up with them. And His voice! Like a resonant bell of finest timbre, never loud but of such penetrating quality that the walls of the room seemed to vibrate with its music.[122]

'Abdu'l-Bahá's exemplary characteristics attracted everyone. Ives remembers an anecdote from when He traveled to Dublin, New Hampshire, as an invited guest of Mrs. Agnes

Parsons:

> The husband of 'Abdu'l-Bahá's hostess in
> Dublin, who, while never becoming an
> avowed believer, had many opportunities of
> meeting and talking with the Master, when
> asked to sum up his impressions of Him,
> responded, after a little consideration: "I think
> He is the most perfect gentleman I have ever
> known."
> Consider. This was the verdict of a man of
> inherited wealth, of wide and profound
> culture, accustomed to judge men by delicate
> standards, and to whom the word "gentleman"
> connoted all which he held most admirable.[123]

One of the most fascinating and provocative
characteristics of 'Abdu'l-Bahá, according to Ives, was His
"ready laughter when alluding to subjects usually approached
with extreme gravity."[124] This account of Ives' final personal
interview with Him on His last day in New York illustrates
'Abdu'l-Bahá's use of laughter:

> I was saying good-bye and my heart was
> sad. Haltingly, I expressed this sorrow that He
> was leaving the country and that, in all
> probability, I should never see Him again. We
> were standing. It was actually the last good-
> bye. 'Abdu'l-Bahá laid His arm across my
> shoulders and walked with me to the door,
> saying that I should be with Him in all the
> worlds of God. And then He laughed—a

hearty, ringing laugh—and I, my eyes blinded with tears, "Why does He laugh?" I thought. Nevertheless, these words, and even more, the tone in which they were uttered, and His joyous laughter, have been an illuminating light upon my path through all these years.[125]

No one could quite comprehend the mystical effect of 'Abdu'l-Bahá's divine voice. Ives has this anecdote of 'Abdu'l-Bahá's last hours in New York City. Crowds of friends had gathered to bid farewell to Him before He left for Europe. Ives remembers:

And then He spoke. For the last time, in this world, that beloved voice resounded in my ears. I have often mentioned the quality of that voice. Never shall it be forgotten by those who truly heard it. It has a bell-like resonance unapproached by any other. It seemed to carry with it the music of another world. Almost one could imagine an accompaniment of unseen choirs.[126]

However, Ives' communication with the Master continued by mail, and sometimes he received responses at unexpected times. For example, Ives had sent a letter to 'Abdu'l-Bahá after His trip to Dublin, New Hampshire, and had not expected a reply. Imagine his surprise and delight upon receipt of a Tablet from 'Abdu'l-Bahá in 1912! Ives said that the significance of the following words became apparent to him many years later:

Written from Malden, Mass., August 26, 1912:

"O thou, my revered friend:

Your letter imparted the utmost rejoicing, for its contents evidenced attraction to the Kingdom of God and enkindlement with the Fire of the Love of God!

A hundred thousand ministers have come and gone: they left behind no trace nor fruit, nor were their lives productive.

To be fruitless in the world of humanity is the manifest loss. A wise person will not attach his heart to ephemeral things: nay, rather, will he continually seek immortal life and strive to obtain eternal happiness.

Now, praise be to God that thou has turned thy face towards the Kingdom, and art aspiring to receive Divine Bestowals from the Realm of Might.

I have become hopeful, and prayed that thou mayest attain to another Bounty; seek another Life; ask for another World; draw nearer unto God; become informed of the Mysteries of the Kingdom; attain to Life Eternal and become encircled with the Glory Everlasting.

Upon thee be the Glory of the Most Glorious."

(Signed) 'Abdu'l-Bahá 'Abbas.[127]

Closing

The foregoing are just a few drops from the boundless ocean of virtues and admirable qualities and characteristics of the Master. Stories about 'Abdu'l-Bahá's divine example from the experiences of two Easterners and two Westerners were shared. Only a few of the myriad of remembrances written by these devoted believers who were affected by the character, words, and deeds of the Master could be included in this compilation.

As reflected in these memories, 'Abdu'l-Bahá's life was truly that of a spiritual master. Those persons whose paths He crossed were deeply affected by His love regardless of their age, nationality, religion, and background. The styles used by these four chroniclers to record their experiences may have been different, the scenes they witnessed may have been varied, and the embellishments of memories may have been unique to each of them, but all were captivated by His heavenly and majestic qualities.

The most effective way to share the healing message of Bahá'u'lláh is by following the example of 'Abdu'l-Bahá, the Perfect Exemplar. He was filled with joy and his life was dedicated to service. It is hoped that, as a result of the perusal of these memoirs, 'Abdu'l-Bahá's life will become a source of inspiration to the reader and that a deeper understanding of the teachings of the Bahá'í Faith through the example of 'Abdu'l-Bahá may be attained.

Howard Colby Ives summarizes the earthly life of the Master in these sweet words:

> Here I saw a man who, outwardly, like myself, lived in the world of confusion, yet, inwardly, beyond the possibility of doubt, lived and worked in that higher and real world. All His concepts, all His motives, all His actions, derived their springs from that "World of Light." And, which is to me a most inspiring and encouraging fact, He took it for granted that you and I, the ordinary run-of-the mill humanity, could enter into and live and move in that world if we would.[128]

Ives ends his memoirs by saying:

> To those who have read this chronicle with the "eye of heart" some glimmer of conviction may have come that such a world is open to them, such a life may be approximated for themselves, such a portal may be entered by

their feet, such a freedom be attained. It is
with this hope that my story has been told.[129]

It is the wish of this servant, the author, that these
memories will open the door for readers to follow the
footsteps of 'Abdu'l-Bahá and emulate His example in deeds
and actions.[130]

Bibliography

'Abdu'l-Bahá. *A Traveler's Narrative,* vol. 2. Trans. by E. G. Browne. Amsterdam: Philo Press, 1891.

Blomfield, Lady (Sitárih Khánum). *The Chosen Highway.* IL: Bahá'í Publishing Trust, 1967.

"From Badi Bushrui's Notes," in *Payám-i-Bahá'í,* no. 251, Oct. 2000, 8-10.

"From Badi Bushrui's Notes," in *Payám-i-Bahá'í,* nos. 273-274, Aug.-Sept., 2002, 7-9.

"Habíb Mu'ayyad (Habíbu'lláh <u>Kh</u>udába<u>kh</u>sh)." *The Bahá'í World 1968-1973.* Vol. 15, Haifa: Bahá'í World Centre, 1976, 501-503.

"Howard Colby Ives." In Memoriam, *The Bahá'í World 1940-1944.* Vol. 9, Wilmette IL: Bahá'í Publishing Committee, 1945, 608-613.

Ives, Howard Colby. *Portals to Freedom.* New York: E. P. Dutton and Company, 1937.

Metelmann, Velda Piff. *Lua Getsinger: Herald of the Covenant.* Oxford: George Ronald, 1997.

"Mírzá Badí Bushru'í." *The Bahá'í World 1968-1973*. Haifa: Bahá'í World Centre, 1976, vol. 15, 545-547.

Muayyad, Hábíb. *Kháṭirát Hábíb*, vol. 1. Hofheim, Germany: Bahá'í-Verlag, reprinted, 1998.

Mu'ayyid, *Kháterát Habib*, vol. 2. Tihrán: Mú'assesih Millí Matbú'át Amrí, 129 Badii [1974].

Mú'ayyad, Habib. *Eight Years Near 'Abdu'l-Bahá: The Diary of Dr. Habib Mú'ayyad*. Translated and annotated by Ahang Rabbani, Witnesses to Báb and Bahá'í History, 2007.

Parsons, Agnes, ed. Richard Hollinger. *'Abdu'l-Bahá in America: Agnes Parsons' Diary*. Los Angeles: Kalimát Press, 1996.

"Sitarih Khanum (Sara, Lady Blomfield)." *The Bahá'í World 1938-1940*. Wilmette, IL: Bahá'í Publishing Committee, 1942, vol. 8, 651-656.

Taherzadeh, Adib. *The Covenant of Bahá'u'lláh*. Oxford: George Ronald, 1992.

Thompson, Juliet. *The Diary of Juliet Thompson*, with Preface by Marzieh Gail. Los Angeles: Kalimát Press, 1983.

Weinberg, Robert. *The First Obligation - Lady Blomfield and the Save the Children Fund,* http://users.whsmithnet.co.uk/ispalin/heritage/scf.htm

Unpublished notes of Badi Bushrui from his family's collection.

Suggested Readings

'Abdu'l-Bahá. *'Abdu'l-Bahá in London: Addresses and Notes of Conversations*. Bahá'í Publishing Trust, reprinted 1982.

_____ *Memorials of the Faithful*. Wilmette, IL: Bahá'í Publishing Trust, 1971.

_____ *Paris Talks: Addresses Given by 'Abdu'l-Bahá in 1911*. London: The Bahá'í Publishing Trust, 1995.

_____ *Selections from the Writings of 'Abdu'l-Bahá*. Compiled by the Research Department of the Universal House of Justice and translated by a Committee at the Bahá'í World Centre and by Marzieh Gail. Haifa: Bahá'í World Centre, 1978.

_____ *Some Answered Questions*. Compiled by Laura Clifford Barney. Delhi: Prabhat Offset Press, 1973.

_____ *The Secret of Divine Civilization*. Trans. Marzieh Gail. Wilmette, IL: Bahá'í Publishing Trust, 1982.

_____ *The Promulgation of Universal Peace: Talks Delivered by 'Abdu'l-Bahá during His Visit to the United States and Canada in 1912*. Compiled by Howard MacNutt.

Wilmette, IL: Bahá'í Publishing Trust, 1982.

Afroukhteh, Dr Youness. *Memories of Nine Years in 'Akká*. Oxford: George Ronald, reprinted, 2005.

Ahdieh, Hussein and Elaine A. Hopson. *'Abdu'l-Bahá in New York: The City of the Covenant*. New York: The Spiritual Assembly of the Bahá'ís of New York, 1987.

Balyuzi, H. M. *'Abdu'l-Bahá: The Centre of the Covenant*. Oxford: George Ronald, 1971.

Browne, Romona Allen. *Memories of 'Abdu'l-Bahá: Recollections of the Early Days of the Bahá'í Faith in California*. Wilmette, IL: Bahá'í Publishing Trust, 1980.

Chase, Thornton. *In Galilee*. Los Angeles: Kalimát Press, reprint, 1985.

Cobb, Stanwood. *Memories of 'Abdu'l-Bahá*. Washington, DC: Avalon, n.d. 1962.

Goodall, Helen S. and Ella Goodall Cooper. *Daily Lessons Received at 'Akká, January 1908*. Wilmette, IL: Bahá'í Publishing Trust, 1979.

Hogenson, Kathryn Jewett. *Lighting the Western Sky: The Hearst Pilgrimage and the Establishment of the Bahá'í Faith in the West*. Oxford: George Ronald, 2010.

Honnold, Annamarie, ed. *Vignettes from the Life of 'Abdu'l-Bahá*. Oxford: George Ronald, 1982.

Maxwell, May. *An Early Pilgrimage*. Haverhill, Suffolk: Lowe & Brydone, 1917. Rev.ed. Oxford: George Ronald, 1969.

Mírzá Mahmúd-i-Zarqání. *Mahmúd's Diary*. Trans. Mohi Sobhani with the assistance of Shirley Macias. Oxford: George Ronald, 1998.

Nakhjavani, Violette. *The Maxwells of Montreal: Early Years*

1870-1922. Oxford: George Ronald, 2011.

Parson, Agnes. Richard Hollinger, ed. *'Abdu'l-Bahá in America: Agnes Parsons' Diary.* Los Angeles: Kalimát Press, 1966.

Stockman, Robert. *'Abdu'l-Bahá in America.* Wilmette, IL: Bahá'í Publishing Trust, 2012.

Thompson, Juliet. *The Diary of Juliet Thompson.* Los Angeles: Kalimát Press, 1983.

Townshend, George. *'Abdu'l-Bahá: The Master.* Oxford: George Ronald, 1987.

Ward, Allan. *239 Days: 'Abdu'l-Bahá's Journey in America.* Chicago, IL: Bahá'í Publishing Trust, 1979.

Weinberg, Robert. *Ethel Jenner Rosenberg: The Life and Times of England's Outstanding Bahá'í Pioneer Worker.* Oxford: George Ronald, 1995.

Wilhelm, Roy and Stanwood Cobb and Genevieve Coy. *In His Presence: Visits to 'Abdu'l-Bahá.* Los Angeles: Kalimát Press, 1989.

Notes and References

1- See 'Abdu'l-Bahá, *Promulgation of Universal Peace* (Wilmette, IL: Bahá'í Publishing Trust, 1982); 'Abdu'l-Bahá, *Paris Talks: Addresses Given by 'Abdu'l-Bahá in 1911* (London: The Bahá'í Publishing Trust, 1995); and H. M. Balyuzi, *'Abdu'l-Bahá* (Oxford: George Ronald, 1992).

2- Acre or `Akkā (Akko; Arabic: عكّا `Akkā) is a city in the Western Galilee region of northern Israel, on the northern extremity of Haifa Bay. Acre is one of the oldest continuously inhabited sites in the country. 'Akká will be used throughout this book. The son of the prophet-founder of the Bahá'í Faith, 'Abdu'l-Bahá, (Abbás Effendi), was a prisoner of the Ottomans when the first Bahá'í pilgrims from the western world arrived in 'Akká in 1898.

3- See Suggested Readings at the back. In this compilation, Badi Bushrui and Habib Moayyad will be the accepted transliterated spelling of names of Badí' Bushrú'í and Habíb Mu'ayyad.

4- The title "Central Figure of the Faith" refers to 'Abdu'l-Bahá.

5- Agnes Parsons, *Agnes Parsons' Diary*, Foreword by Sandra

Hutchinson, xi.

6- "Notes from Badi Bushrui," in *Payám-i-Bahá'í*, Nos. 273-274, Aug-Sept., 2002, 7.

7- See Mona Khademi, *Sefaat Malakouti: Negahi be shakhsiyat hazrat 'Abdu'l-Bahá* (Los Angeles: Sherkat Ketab, 2012).

8- "Prophet of Peace Comes to Buffalo," in *Buffalo New York Times*, Sept. 10, 1912. "Abdul Baha, The Baha'i Prophet, Speaks at Stanford University," in *Palo Altan*, Nov. 1, 1912.

9- 'Abdu'l-Bahá, *A Traveler's Narrative*, trans. E. G. Browne, vol. 2 (Amsterdam: Philo Press, 1891), xxxvi.

10- "Mírzá Badí' Bushrū'í," In Memoriam, *The Bahá'í World*, 1968-1973, vol. 15, 545.

11- "Notes of Badi Bushrui," in *Payám-i-Bahá'í*, nos. 273-274, 2002, 7-8.

12- "Mírzá Badí' Bushrū'í," In Memoriam, *The Bahá'í World*, 1968-1973, vol. 15, 545.

13- Shoghi Effendi (1897-1957), a grandson of 'Abdu'l-Bahá, became the Guardian of the Bahá'í Faith in 1921 and in this capacity served as the head of the Faith.

14- "Notes of Badi Bushrui," in *Payám-i-Bahá'í*, nos. 273-274, 2002, 7-8. Mishkín-Qalam was a prominent Bahá'í and a famous calligrapher of nineteenth-century Persia.

15- The name of Syrian Protestant College was changed to American University in 1922.

16- Ibid., 8. Mirza Haydar 'Ali was a leading Bahá'í and a trusted disciple of Bahá'u'lláh.

17- "Mírzá Badí' Bushrū'í," In Memoriam, *The Bahá'í World* 1968-1973, vol. 15, 546.

18- Ibid., 547.

19- Mírzá Mihdí (1848–1870) is the youngest son of Bahá'u'lláh. He did not survive a fall through a skylight onto a stone floor below.

20- Unpublished notes of Badi Bushrui, November 18, 1957.

21- "Notes of Badi Bushrui," in *Payám-i-Bahá'í*, nos. 273-274, Aug.-Sept. 2002, 8.

22- Unpublished notes of Badi Bushrui, August 3, 1915.

23- "Notes of Badi Busrhui," in *Payám-i-Bahá'í*, no. 208, March 1997, 12.

24- Báb (1819-1850) was the founder of Bábism, the forerunner of Bahá'u'lláh, and one of three central figures of the Bahá'í Faith.

25- "Notes of Badi Bushrui," in *Payám-i-Bahá'í*, nos. 273-274, Aug.-Sept. 2002, 8.

26- Ibid, 9. King of Martyrs was Mírzá Muhammad-Hasan, given the title Sultánu'sh-Shuhada' (King of Martyrs) by Bahá'u'lláh. He was identified as one of the nineteen Apostles of Bahá'u'lláh and was beheaded in 1879 as a result of being Bahá'í.

27- "Notes of Badi Bushrui," in *Payám-i-Bahá'í*, no. 251, Oct. 2000, 9.

28- Ibid, 9.

29- Unpublished notes of Badi Bushrui, October 3, 1915. Lira was the Turkish currency at the time.

30- Unpublished notes of Badi Bushrui.

31- Unpublished notes of Badi Bushrui, November 7, 1915. First day of Muharram is the birth of the Báb (Muharram 1, 1235 AH equivalent to Oct. 20, 1819).

32- Ibid., November 25, 1915.

33- Ibid., November 1, 1915.

34- "Notes of Badi Bushrui," *Payám-i-Bahá'í*, nos. 273-274, 9.

35- Unpublished notes of Badi Bushrui, October 31, 1915.

36- Unpublished notes of Badi Bushrui, November 12, 1915.

37- Ibid.

38- Ibid.

39- Ibid., December 2, 1915.

40- Ibid., August 18, 1915.

41- Kírmánsháh, also written Kermanshah, is a western state in Iran, also known as Bákhtarán.

96 / *Heavenly Attributes*

42- Hamadan, Iran, was the closest big city to Kermanshah.

43- "Habíb Mú'ayyad (Habíbu'lláh Khudábakhsh)," In Memoriam, *The Bahá'í World,* 1968-1973, vol. 15, 501.

44- Habíb Mú'ayyad, *Kháterát-i- Habíb,* vol. 1 (Hofheim, Germany: Bahá'í-Verlag, 1998), p. b.

45- Some significant letters of Bahá'u'lláh and 'Abdu'l-Bahá are referred to as Tablets for their permanencies and timeless nature.

46- Mírzá Abu'l-Fadl-i-Gulpáygání (1844–1914) was the foremost Bahá'í scholar. He was one of the few Apostles of Bahá'u'lláh who never actually met Bahá'u'lláh.

47- Habib Mú'ayyad, *Eight Years Near 'Abdu'l-Bahá: The Diary of Dr. Habíb Mú'ayyad.* Translated and annotated by Ahang Rabbani, Witnesses to Báb and Bahá'í History, 2007, 364.

48- See H. M. Balyuzi, *'Abdu'l-Bahá* (Oxford: George Ronald), 408. Azizu'l lláh Bahádor was a fellow student at the Syrian Protestant College from which Dr. Moayyad had graduated.

49- H. M. Balyuzi, *'Abdu'l-Bahá: The Centre of the Covenant of Bahá'u'lláh* (Oxford: George Ronald, reprinted 1992), 411.

50- Velda Piff Metelmann, *Lua Getsinger: Herald of the Covenant* (Oxford: George Ronald), 310.

51- Mú'ayyad, *Eight Years Near 'Abdu'l-Bahá,* 2.

52- Ibid., 380, ft. 414: Dr. Mú'ayyad adopted this surname, "confirmed," because of the oft-repeated appellation by 'Abdu'l-Bahá.

53- Hábíb Mu'ayyad, *Khátirát Habíb,* vol. 1 (Hofheim, Germany: Bahá'í Verlag, 1998), 260.

54- "Habíb Mu'ayyad (Habíbu'lláh Khudábakhsh)," In Memoriam, *The Bahá'í World,* 1968-1973, vol. 15 (Haifa: Bahá'í World Centre, 1976), 502.

55- Ibid., 502.

56- "Tale of a Persian Rug: West Hall of Curio Was Presented by Iranian Alumnus," *Al-Kulliyah,* vol. 28, no. 4, April 1953 from the American University of Beirut Library (Lebanon). Ahmad Shah Qajar

(1898-1930), the last of Qajar dynasty, was the Shah of Iran from 1909 to 1925.

57- Mú'ayyad, *Eight Years Near 'Abdu'l-Bahá*, 37.

58- See Habíb Mu'ayyad, <u>Khátirát Habíb</u>, 2 vols. (Hofheim, Germany: Bahá'í Verlag, 1996, 2004).

59- Mú'ayyad, *Eight Years Near 'Abdu'l-Bahá*, 135, ft. 156: Founded in the eleventh century CE by the Persian immigrant Hamza Ibn 'Alí Ibn Ahmad, it is a sect of Islam which reveres the Fátimid caliph al-Hakím, and incorporates elements of Christianity and Greek philosophy.

60- Ibid., 135-36.

61- Ibid., 141-42.

62- Ibid., 137, ft. 157: The original refers to the use of the Hyssop (*Hyssopus officinalis*), a member of the mint family.

63- Ibid., 136.

64- Ibid., 187-88.

65- Ibid., 62.

66- Ibid., 97.

67- The Most Exalted Branch refers to 'Abdu'l-Bahá.

68- Ancient Beauty refers to Bahá'u'lláh.

69- Mú'ayyad, *Eight Years Near 'Abdu'l-Bahá*, 192-193.

70- "Saláru'd-Dawlih was a younger brother of Muhammad-Ali Sháh, who had been deposed by the Revolution [in Iran] of 1909. He was a troublesome figure who in 1907 had made a bid for the throne against his brother, and then in 1911, after his brother's deposition, he appeared in the west of Persia with troops to assist his brother in his futile attempt to regain the throne." From *The Bábí and Bahá'í Religions, 1844-1944: Some Contemporary Western Accounts*, edited by Moojan Momen (Oxford; George Ronald, 1981), 458.

71- Mú'ayyad, *Eight Years Near 'Abdu'l-Bahá*, 105-106, ft. 125: Ali Nakhjavani is thanked for the rendering of this poem.

72- Ibid., 107.

73- Ibid., 107.

74- The Great Mystery of God refers to 'Abdu'l-Bahá.

75- Adib Taherzadeh, *The Covenant of Bahá'u'lláh* (Oxford: George Ronald, 1992), 225-226 quoting Dr. Habíb Mu'ayyad, *Kháṭirát-i-Habíb* (Memoirs of Habíb), Tihran: 1961. P. 226, ft: These are not the exact words of 'Abdu'l-Bahá, but they are very close to what He said. (A.T.)

76- Mú'ayyad, *Eight Years Near 'Abdu'l-Bahá*, 394-395.

77- Ibid., 395-96, ft. 437: "Since my examination was taking place during World War I, I did not have access to a laboratory to perform various tests in addition to clinical examination. It so happened that none were needed anyway since in Paris and London, through the insistence of certain Bahá'ís, laboratory tests had been performed and everything was found to be in the normal range." (By Habib Moayyad)

78- Ibid., 285, ft. 325: Ridván and Firdaws Gardens (Habib Mu'ayyad).

79- Ibid., 285.

80- Mu'ayyid, *Kháterát Habib*, vol. 2 (Tihrán: Mú'assesih Millí Matbú'át Amrí, 129 Badii [1974]), 303; provisional by Khazeh Fananapazir.

81- See Suggested Readings.

82- 'Abdu'l-Bahá, *Paris Talks: Addresses Given by 'Abdu'l-Bahá in 1911*, 12th edition (London: The Bahá'í Publishing Trust, 1995), Introduction, xi-xii.

83- Robert Stockman, *The Bahá'í Faith in America: Early Expansion 1900-1912*, vol. 2 (Oxford: George Ronald, 1991), 406.

84- Howard Colby Ives, *Portals to Freedom* (New York: E. P. Dutton, & Company, 1937), 14-15.

85- Ives, *Portal to Freedom*, 39.

86- See Suggested Readings.

87- Arthur Blomfield was the famous architect and son of the Bishop of London.

88- League of Nations is the predecessor of the United Nations.

89- 'Abdu'l-Bahá, *Paris Talks: Addresses Given by 'Abdu'l-Bahá in 1911* (London: The Bahá'í Publishing Trust, 1995), first published in 1912 as *Talks by Abdul Baha Given in Paris* by the Unity Press, East Sheen, Surrey.

90- In Persian, sitárih means star and khánum means lady.

91- "Sitarih Khanum (Sara, Lady Blomfield)," In Memoriam, *The Bahá'í World 1938-1940* (New York: Bahá'í Publishing Committee, 1942), vol. 8, 653.

92- See Lady Blomfield, *The Chosen Highway* (Wilmette, IL: Bahá'í Publishing Trust, 1967).

93- "Sitarih Khanum (Sara, Lady Blomfield)," In Memoriam, *The World,* 1938-1940, vol. 8, 651.

94- Lady Blomfield, *The Chosen Highway,* 149.

95- Ibid., 150.

96- Ibid., 150.

97- Ibid., 157-58.

98- Ibid., 156.

99- Ibid., 161-62.

100- Ibid., 162.

101- Ibid., 157.

102- Ibid., 163.

103- Ibid., 169.

104- Ibid., 166.

105- Ibid., 171.

106- Ibid., 184-85.

107- Ibid., 174.

108- "Howard Colby Ives," In Memoriam, *The Bahá'í World,* 1940-1944, vol. 9, 609.

109- Ives, *Portals to Freedom,* 33.

110- Ibid., 91.

111- "Howard Colby Ives," In Memoriam, *The Bahá'í World,* vol. 9,

611.

112- Ibid., 611.

113- Ibid., 611.

114- Ives, *Portals to Freedom*, 37.

115- Ibid., 39-40.

116- Ibid., 137-38.

117- Ibid., 135-36.

118- Ibid., 95-96.

119- Ibid., 65-66.

120- Ibid., 89-9.

121- Ibid., 194-95.

122- Ibid., 127.

123- Ibid., 116.

124- Ibid., 193.

125- Ibid., 193-94.

126- Ibid., 213.

127- Ibid., 130-31.

128- Ibid., 253.

129- Ibid., 253.

130- The first and last name of the author, Mona Khademi, is literally translated as "the wish of the servant"!